T
World
Football
Jokes

The World's Best Football Jokes

Edward Phillips

ILLUSTRATED BY
GRAHAM MORRIS

HarperCollinsPublishers

HarperCollins*Publishers*
77–85 Fulham Palace Road,
Hammersmith, London W6 8JB

This paperback edition 1993
5 7 9 8 6 4

First published in Great Britain by
Fontana 1991

ISBN 0 00 637962 1

Set in Goudy

Printed and bound in Great Britain by
Caledonian International Book Manufacturing Ltd, Glasgow

ACKNOWLEDGEMENTS

Many people have assisted me with favourite football stories and anecdotes for this book and I should particularly like to thank the following:

Andrew Mitchell, Conservative MP for Gedling (Nottingham); Matthew Sturgis, football writer for the *Independent*; John Motson, BBC sports commentator; Des MacHale, Professor of Mathematics, University College, Cork; Ken Friar, Managing Director, Arsenal FC; John Howarth, Club Secretary, Blackburn Rovers FC; Brian Anderson, Club Secretary, Darlington FC; Bob Twyford, Club Secretary, Bristol Rovers FC; T. F. Newman, Club Secretary, Bradford City FC; Bill Kenyon, Club Secretary, Rochdale FC; George Binns, Club Secretary, and Ken O'Doherty, player, both of Huddersfield Town FC; J. T. Cale, Club Secretary, Oldham Athletic FC; Matthew Chiles, Administration Assistant, West Bromwich Albion FC; Brian Naysmith, Chief Executive, Fulham FC; John Adams, Vice-Chairman and Vic Jobson, Chairman, both of Southend United FC; R. Briggs of R. J. S. Programmes, Cleethorpes.

I am also grateful to *Private Eye* for giving me permission to use the extracts from the 'Colemanballs' series of commentators' gaffes.

'It's a funny old game, football,' as the captain said to the manager after his team had been trounced 6—0 in an important relegation match.

To which the manager replied grimly, 'Yes – but it isn't meant to be!'

What is football? It has been described as a game with twenty-two players, two linesmen and 20,000 referees.

One of the most famous footballers of all time is the legendary Stanley Matthews, who played for Blackpool and Stoke City at outside-right. It was said of him that he was so fast that when he went to bed at night, he could turn out the light at the bedroom door and be under the blankets before the room got dark.

A Scottish captain once lent the referee a coin for the toss and demanded his whistle as security.

Why do Pakistanis make very poor footballers? Every time you give them a corner they open a shop on it.

A desperate manager, whose team had lost fourteen consecutive games, rang a colleague for advice on training methods.

'I'll tell you what you should do,' said his friend. 'Take the team out on a six-mile run every day.'

'What's the point of that?' asked the manager.

'Today's Monday,' was the reply. 'By Saturday, they'll be thirty-six miles away and you can forget all about them!'

The manager of a club way down at the bottom of the Fourth Division placed eleven dustbins in formation on the pitch and had his team practise dribbling around them and passing between them before shooting for goal. After just one session he had to abandon this method of training for reasons of team morale: the dustbins won 6—0.

A match between two non-League teams took place last winter in the North of England. It had been raining heavily all week and the ground resembled a swamp. However, the referee ruled that play was possible and tossed the coin to determine ends. The visiting captain won the toss and, after a moment's thought, said, 'OK – we'll take the shallow end!'

The following instruction recently appeared on the notice-board of a large car factory in Cowley: ALL APPLICATIONS FOR LEAVE OF ABSENCE FOR FAMILY BEREAVEMENTS, SICKNESS, JURY DUTY, ETC., MUST BE HANDED IN TO THE PERSONNEL MANAGER NO LATER THAN 6 P.M. ON THE DAY PRECEDING THE MATCH.

A goalkeeper had had a particularly bad season and announced that he was retiring from professional football. In a television interview he was asked his reasons for quitting the game. 'Well, basically,' he said, 'it's a question of illness and fatigue.'

'Can you be more specific?' asked the interviewer.

'Well,' said the player, 'specifically the fans are sick and tired of me.'

Over breakfast one morning, a little boy kept staring intently at his grandfather. 'Is anything the matter, son?' the old man asked.

'No, Gramps. I was just wondering what position you play in the football team.'

'What are you talking about?' laughed Gramps. 'I'm far too old to play football.'

'Oh,' said the little boy. 'It's just that Dad said that when you kicked off, we'd be able to afford a new car.'

In a particularly rough tackle, a player was knocked unconscious. A first-aid man ran over and began to sprinkle water in his face and fan him with a towel. Slowly the player recovered consciousness and said groggily, 'How the hell do they expect us to play in all this wind and rain?'

One Friday afternoon, late last season, a leading member of a big First Division club was tragically knocked down and killed by a hit-and-run driver. One of the reserves, seeing a chance to get a game at last, approached the coach and asked, 'Do you think I could take his place, boss?'

'That's a good idea,' replied the coach. 'I'll see if I can arrange it with the undertaker.'

A football widow decided to take an interest in the game in order to share her husband's pastime. One Saturday afternoon she accompanied him to the local match. It was a good game: plenty of open play, good attacking movements and strong defence. She was enjoying the game when suddenly all the players except one froze and stood like statues. The active player grabbed the ball and shoved it up his jersey.

Then he too remained motionless. The woman looked at the referee to see what action he was going to take, but he too was in a statue-like position.

'Whatever are they doing?' she asked.

'Oh, they're posing for the "Spot-the-Ball" competition,' replied her husband.

An American visitor to England watched his very first football match and was struck by the differences between English and American football. After the match he fell into conversation with one of the English players and remarked, 'You know, over in the States, our players wear thick protective clothing. You guys must be frozen stiff in those light clothes.'

'It's not so bad,' said the Englishman. 'Sometimes the ground is covered in snow.'

'You don't say!' exclaimed the American. 'What do you do about the balls? Paint them red?'

'Oh, no,' said the player. 'We just wear an extra pair of shorts.'

A Fourth Division coach was addressing his team during a training session. 'Now, lads,' he said, 'over the last few months, I've given you a lot of tips and advice on passing, dribbling, kicking and defensive play.' The team nodded appreciatively. 'Well, you can forget it all,' said the coach, 'because we've just sold the bloody lot of you!'

A well-known footballer and his wife recently decided to take a holiday at a nudist camp. He was asked to referee the camp football match but, surprisingly, he declined the offer. 'Why did you refuse to referee that match?' asked his wife.

'I wasn't too happy about where I had to carry the spare whistle,' replied the husband.

There was once a match in Liverpool between Anglican vicars and Roman Catholic priests. Early in the game the Catholics were awarded a penalty. Father Flanagan placed the ball carefully, took a long run at it, and kicked. The ball sailed high into the air and missed the goal by miles. Father Flanagan didn't utter a word. He just stood there with a grim expression on his face. The team captain, Monsignor Ryan, came up behind him and said reprovingly, 'Father, that is the most profane silence I have ever heard!'

It was the last game of the season. Mathieson had been with the team from the start but he was such a slow and clumsy player that never once had he actually been allowed to play, but had spent all his time on the substitute bench. At this last match, however, there were so many fouls and injuries that every substitute but him had been sent on. With ten minutes to go, yet another player was carried off the field and the coach looked at the substitute bench, his eye finally alighting on Mathieson. Mathieson's face lit up. 'Are you going to send me on, coach?' he asked eagerly.

'No!' snapped the coach. 'Just get out of the way. I'm going to send in the bench!'

The reigning Miss World – from Brazil – was invited to start a charity football match by performing the ceremonial kick-off. After an excellent game, which raised a great deal of money, a dinner was held. During the speeches which followed, Miss World made the evening for all present when, in broken English and with great charm, she said, 'It eez great honour for me to kick off your ball; I will be pleased to come back any time to English football clubs and kick all your balls off.'

Did you hear about the England international player who had a date with a referee's daughter? She penalised him three times – for handling, interference and trying to pull off a jersey.

Referees at Celtic Rangers matches always have a particularly hard time. One poor unfortunate, officiating at his first fixture, was checking in with the team managers before the kick-off. 'Well, that seems to be about everything,' said the Rangers boss. 'Now, if you'd just like to give us the name and address of your next-of-kin, we can start the match.'

A player was being ticked off by the coach for missing a very easy goal-kick. 'All right,' said the player, 'how *should* I have played the shot?'
'Under an assumed name,' snapped the coach.

The football club dance was in full swing when three strangers arrived and demanded admission. 'May I see your tickets, please?' said the club secretary at the door.

'We haven't got any tickets,' said one of the men. 'We're friends of the referee.'

'Get out of here!' said the club secretary. 'Whoever heard of a referee with three friends!'

'When I started as a commentator,' says John Motson, 'I was bombarded by letters from an irate viewer in the north who resented my reference to the colour of shirts which teams were wearing. His point was that he came from a working-class family who could not afford colour television, and was fed up with being told who was in the red shirts or the green shirts, when he had no way of identifying them. Determined to do something to pacify him, I waited for a quiet moment in a match at Roker Park, and then came out with a remark I have never been allowed to forget! "For those watching in black-and-white," I said, "Spurs are in the yellow shirts!" '

John once received a letter from the Race Relations Board when, after a particularly good goal by Watford, he said, 'There's a case of Barnes doing the spade-work for Blissett!' He adds that he didn't intend this remark to come out the way it did – although nobody laughed louder than the black players themselves!

Another well-known television sports commentator, who shall be nameless, was talking to his friends in the pub one night. 'It's amazing,' he said. 'I've been in the business for twenty years and it just occurred to me today that I don't know anything about the game at all!'

'Well, why don't you give it up then?' asked a bystander.

'I can't,' replied the commentator. 'I've become a world authority!'

THE BEST OF 'COLEMANBALLS'

'Their manager, Terry Neil, isn't here today, which suggests he is elsewhere.' (Brian Moore)

'With the very last kick of the game, Bobby McDonald scored with a header.' (Alan Parry)

'Well, it's Ipswich nil, Liverpool two, and if that's the way the score stays then you've got to fancy Liverpool to win.' (Peter Jones)

'Bolton are on the crest of a slump.' (Anon)

'You couldn't have counted the number of moves Alan Ball made . . . I counted four and possibly five.' (John Motson)

'When one team scores early in the game, it often takes an early lead.' (Pat Marsden)

'And Meade had a hat-trick. He scored two goals.' (Richard Whitmore)

'I am a firm believer that if you score one goal, the other team have to score two to win.' (Howard Wilkinson)

'Ian Rush unleashed his left foot and it hit the back of the net.' (Mike England)

'It will be a shame if either side lose. And that applies to both sides.' (Jock Brown)

'It was a good match which could have gone either way and very nearly did.' (Jim Sherwin)

'He had an eternity to play that ball, but he took too long over it.' (Martin Tyler)

'Everything in our favour was against us.' (Danny Blanchflower)

'Nearly all the Brazilian players are wearing yellow shirts. It's a fabulous kaleidoscope of colour.' (John Motson)

'And so they have not been able to improve on their hundred percent record.' (Sports Roundup)

The Oxford and Cambridge University student teams were due to play when one of the Oxford men had to drop out at short notice. 'Why don't we use Johnson, the head porter at Balliol?' suggested the Oxford captain to the selection committee. 'I've seen him play in a local amateur team and he's a brilliant striker – absolutely unstoppable. We can get him a set of colours and as long as he doesn't speak to anyone, we should be able to get away with it.'

The committee thought this might be a little unethical but in desperation they agreed to the plan. They rigged out the Balliol porter and put him on the left wing. He was, as the Oxford captain had said, unstoppable, and they beat Cambridge 9—1, Johnson having scored eight of the goals single-handed.

Afterwards in the bar, the Cambridge captain approached Johnson and said sportingly, 'Well done, old boy! A magnificent effort! By the way, what are you studying at Balliol?'

The porter thought for a moment, then said brightly, 'Sums!'

One of the lesser-known stories in Greek mythology tells of a classic football match on Mount Olympus between the Gods and the Mortals. The Gods trounced the Mortals 8—0 and attributed their victory to the brilliance of their new centaur-forward.

A First Division reserves team recently played against a side made up of long-term prisoners from Strangeways. (The Strangeways team were playing at home, of course!) The game had only been in progress for about ten minutes when the referee noticed that the prison team were fielding twelve men. Blowing his whistle angrily, he called the Strangeways captain over and said, 'What the hell's the idea of having twelve men on the field? Don't you know that's illegal?'

'Well,' said the captain, unabashed, 'you know us – we cheat!'

A First Division player not noted for his modesty was regaling his friends in the local pub. 'I came out of the ground after the match last Saturday and there were literally hundreds of fans outside waving autograph books at me!' Noticing the sceptical looks on the faces of his listeners, he added, 'It's quite true! If you don't believe me, ask Kenny Dalglish – he was standing right next to me!'

The rather unpopular secretary of a Fourth Division club was recently rushed to hospital with a suspected duodenal ulcer. The next day he received a get-well card from the club committee with the postscript: 'The decision to send you this card was carried by six votes to four, with two abstentions.'

Wife: 'Football, football, football! That's all you ever think about! If you said you were going to stay at home one Saturday afternoon to help with the housework, I think I'd drop dead from the shock!'
Husband: 'It's no good trying to bribe me, dear.'

At a local derby between Arsenal and Spurs last season, a spectator suddenly found himself in the thick of dozens of flying bottles. 'There's nothing to worry about, lad,' said the elderly chap standing next to him. 'It's like the bombs during the war. You won't get hit unless the bottle's got your name on it.'

'That's just what I'm worried about,' said the fan. 'My name's Johnny Walker!'

Reporter: 'Tell me, Mr Harris, will your £100,000 win on the football pools make any difference to your way of life?'

Pools winner: 'None at all. I shall carry on exactly as before.'

Reporter: 'But what about all the begging letters?'

Pools winner: 'Oh, I'll keep sending them out as usual.'

In a crucial Cup semi-final a few years ago, the capacity crowd of 30,000 watched a rather diminutive striker get possession of the ball early in the second half. He was immediately tackled by three large defenders, and went down under a pile of thrashing arms and legs. Emerging dazed from the mêlée a few moments later, he looked round at the crowded stands and gasped, 'How did they all get back in their seats so quickly?'

A famous international footballer was asked to appear nude in the centrefold of a glossy new women's magazine. 'Our intention is to photograph you standing nude holding a ball,' said the features editor.

'I see,' said the footballer. 'What will I be doing with my other hand?'

The match was over and the team captain, who had muffed three easy goal shots, came over to the manager and said, 'You'll have to excuse me if I dash off, chief. I've got a plane to catch and I don't want to miss it.'

'Off you go, then,' said the manager. 'And better luck with the plane.'

The angry captain snarled at the referee. 'What would happen if I called you a blind bastard who couldn't make a correct decision to save his life?'

'It would be a red card for you.'

'And if I didn't say it but only thought it?'

'That's different. If you only thought it but didn't say it, I couldn't do a thing.'

'Well, we'll leave it like that, then, shall we?' smiled the captain.

'I hear you're from Wakefield. Does your town boast a football team?'

'We have a team, yes, but it's nothing to boast about.'

Striker: 'I've just had a good idea for strengthening the team.'

Manager: 'Good! When are you leaving?'

'We've got the best football team in the country – unbeaten and no goals scored against us!'

'How many games have you played?'

'The first one's next Saturday.'

A supporter arrived at the ground one Saturday to find the place completely empty. He went to the office and asked an official, 'What time does the match start?'

'There's no match today,' replied the official.

'But there must be!' argued the fan. 'It's Saturday.'

'I'm telling you there's no match today,' repeated the official.

'But there's always a match on Saturday afternoon,' said the fan, 'even if it's only a reserves game.'

'Watch my lips,' shouted the irate official. 'There is no M–A–T–F–C–H today!'

'Well, for your information,' the would-be spectator shouted back, 'there's no F in match.'

'That's what I've been trying to tell you!' yelled the official.

A man went off to a football match one Saturday afternoon, and while he was away his wife was visited by a 'friend' who just happened to be jogging past her house and was dressed in shorts and singlet. The wife was happily entertaining him on the sofa when suddenly they heard her husband coming through the front door. Quick as a flash, the visitor hid behind the large television set in the corner. The husband came in and said, 'It's started to pour with rain so I thought I'd come home and watch the second half on telly.' He switched on the television and settled down to watch the game. After about twenty minutes the wife's visitor started to get severe cramp so, casting caution to the winds, he calmly got up from behind the set and walked out of the room. The husband turned to his wife and said, 'That's funny – I didn't see the ref send him off.'

It is said that in Ireland, if it looks like rain before a match, they play the extra time first.

'Is your new striker fast?'
'Is he fast! He's so fast, the rest of the team have to run twice as fast just to keep up with him!'

Paddy: 'I couldn't get to the match last Saturday. What was the score?'
Mick: 'Nil–nil.'
Paddy: 'What was it at half-time?'

The manager and coach of an Irish team were discussing the players they had on their books and the manager asked, 'How many goals has O'Halloran scored this season?'
'Exactly double what he scored last season,' replied the coach. 'Eleven.'

'I just don't understand it,' an Irish footballer complained. 'One match I play very well, then the next match I'm terrible.'
'Well,' said his wife, 'why don't you just play every other match?'

'I don't care about results!' said an Irish team manager being interviewed on television. 'Just so long as our team wins!'

Two Irish team managers promised their players a pint of Guinness for every goal they scored during an important match. The final score was 119—98.

In the heat of the game, one of the players threw a vicious punch. The victim was all set to get stuck into him when the referee rushed up and held him back. 'Now then, O'Hara! You know you mustn't retaliate!'

'Come on, ref!' said O'Hara. 'He retaliated first!'

Three football codes prevail in Ireland: Rugby, which is defined as a thugs' game played by gentlemen; soccer – a gentleman's game played by thugs; and Gaelic football – a thugs' game played by thugs!

Two old men were holding up the queue outside the turnstyle before the game, while one of them hunted for his ticket. He looked in his coat pockets and his waistcoat pockets and his trouser pockets, all to no avail. 'Hang on a minute,' said the gateman. 'What's that in your mouth?' It was the missing ticket!

As they moved inside his mate said, 'Crikey, Cyril! You must be getting senile in your old age. Fancy having your ticket in your mouth and forgetting about it!'

'I'm not *that* stupid,' said old Cyril. 'I was chewing last week's date off it.'

The manager of an Irish club was talking to a young player who had applied for a trial with the club. 'Do you kick with both feet?' asked the manager.

'Don't be silly!' said the trialist. 'If I did that, I wouldn't be able to stand up, would I?'

The rivalry between Celtic and Rangers in Scotland is well known. A Celtic fan looking for trouble went up to a perfect stranger in a pub in Sauchiehall Street and shouted in his ear: 'To hell with the Rangers!'

The stranger looked puzzled. 'I don't know what you're talking about, bud,' he said. 'I'm an American from Houston, Texas.'

The Celtic fan looked nonplussed for a moment but then, with a flash of inspiration, he yelled, 'To hell with the Texas Rangers, then!'

'My wife told me last week that she'd leave me if I didn't stop spending so much time at football matches.'

'What a shame!'

'Yes. I shall miss her.'

In church one Sunday the vicar opened his Bible to read the lesson. In a loud voice he proclaimed, 'Corinthians 7!'

A keen football fan who was dozing in the front row woke up with a start and shouted, 'Who were they playing?'

'We're starting up an amateur football team. Would you like to join?'

'I would, yes, but I'm afraid I don't know the first thing about football.'

'That's all right. We need a referee as well.'

After considerable effort and expense a First Division manager succeeded in obtaining the services of Miodrag Krivokapic and Mixu Paatelainen of Dundee, Dariusz Wdowczwk of Celtic, Detzi Kruszynski of Wimbledon, and Steve Ogrizovic of Coventry. 'Are these boys any good?' asked a colleague.

'I couldn't care less,' said the manager. 'I just want to get my own back on some of these smart-aleck TV sports commentators!'

The Football Association was considering a scheme for simplifying club badges and emblems so that they more closely reflected the clubs' names. A committee was set up to receive suggestions and, after a few weeks, the chairman called a meeting. 'Gentlemen,' he said, 'our request for new club badge designs has produced a very satisfactory response. Most of the suggestions are perfectly straightforward and logical – an ox for Oxford United, a sun for Sunderland, a heart for Heart of Midlothian, a windmill and a brick wall for Millwall. However, I'm afraid we must definitely draw the line at the proposed design received from Arsenal!'

'**I**s your goalkeeper getting any better?'
'Not really. Last Saturday he let in five goals in the first ten minutes. He was so fed up when he failed to stop the fifth that he put his head in his hands – and dropped it!'

As the defender ran in to tackle he took a full-blooded kick between the legs and fell unconscious to the ground. When he regained consciousness he was in hospital. He beckoned to the doctor and croaked, 'Is it bad?'

'I'm afraid so,' said the doctor.

'Are my playing days over?' asked the anxious footballer.

'Not necessarily,' answered the medic.

'So will I be able to play football for my club again?'

'Oh yes,' said the doctor, 'providing your club has a ladies team.'

'**J**ust a minute, ref!' yelled the goalkeeper. 'That wasn't a goal!'

'Oh, wasn't it?' shouted the referee. 'You just watch the "Sports Report" on television tonight!'

A big First Division team was very anxious to sign up a certain top-class player. However, nothing they offered would induce him to sign and in desperation they stooped to more underhand methods. The team manager sent his secretary – blonde, 5'2", 38—22—36 – to try to persuade the reluctant striker to sign up. To his surprise, he heard nothing from the girl for over a week. Then one morning she walked into his office and said, 'I've got good news and bad news for you, boss. The good news is – he's ready to sign. The bad news is – he's more than two stone down from his playing weight!'

A footballer was having a lot of trouble with his teeth so he went to see his dentist. 'What's the verdict?' he asked, after the dentist had carried out an examination.

'I forecast eight draws,' said the dentist.

It is said that the manager of a sports equipment company recently approached Nigel Spink, Aston Villa's goalkeeper and asked, 'For £20,000, would you endorse our football boots?'

'For £20,000,' said Nigel, 'I'd even *wear* your football boots!'

'Your team's rubbish! We beat you 9—2 last Saturday, even though we had a man short!'

'What do you mean "a man short"? You had ten players and the referee, didn't you?'

One of the top players in the 1990 England World Cup team was called as a character witness in a matrimonial case and, on being asked his profession, replied, 'I am the greatest footballer in the world!'

After the case was over he came in for a good deal of teasing from his team-mates. 'How could you stand up in court and say a thing like that?' they asked.

'Well,' he replied, 'you must remember I was under oath!'

A match took place recently in Oxford between a local amateur team and a side made up of university tutors and professors. Before the match the two captains faced each other while the referee flipped the coin to decide who would have choice of ends. The local team won the toss and, as the captain shook hands with his opposite number, he said sportingly,

'May the best team win!'

The university captain, a professor of English, replied, 'You mean, may the *better* team win!'

A football hooligan appeared in court charged with disorderly conduct and assault. The arresting officer, giving evidence, stated that the accused had thrown something into the canal. 'What exactly was it that he threw into the canal?' asked the magistrate.

'Stones, sir.'

'Well, that's hardly an offence is it?'

'It was in this case, sir,' said the police officer. 'Stones was the referee.'

Did you hear about the football captain in a minor league who was offered £1,000 to lose a game? It would have been against his principle to take the money but £1,000 against his principle looked pretty good so he took it.

A famous soccer international was talking to another guest at a party. 'I've been persuaded to write my autobiography,' he said, 'but I don't want it published until after I'm dead.'

'Really?' said the guest. 'I shall look forward to reading it.'

'You're all feet!' yelled the coach at the practice session. 'All bloody feet! How many times have I told you – use your brains, use your feet, but let the ball do the work!'

'Well, don't tell me,' shouted the unfortunate player. 'Tell the bloody ball!'

At a recent Irish League match between Newry and Larne, the visitors were awarded a penalty and the captain summoned his best player and said, 'I want you to take this one, Patrick. Just think hard as you kick – think which way the wind is blowing, and think which direction the keeper's going to jump.'

'Holy Mother!' said Patrick. 'Do you expect me to think and kick at the same time?'

'So you want to join us here at Leyton Orient as a goal-keeper, do you? What sort of salary were you expecting?'

'£500 a week.'

'And what experience have you had?'

'I've never played in goal before.'

'You've no goalkeeping experience and you want £500 a week!'

'Well, it's much harder when you don't know anything about it.'

Some years ago an important European match between England and Scotland was taking place in Milan. The referee was Hungarian. His command of English left a good deal to be desired and the players of both teams were taking the mickey out of him at every opportunity. Finally the Hungarian's patience ran out. 'You British!' he shouted. 'You think I know damn nothing about the game! Let me tell you – I know damn all!'

A big interdenominational football match was due to take place one Saturday between a team of Catholic priests and a team of rabbis. On the preceding Monday, disaster struck the Catholics. Their star player broke his leg! 'What are we going to do?' said Monsignor O'Reilly, the priests' manager.

'Well,' said Father O'Neal hesitantly, 'I know this is a little unethical, but Gary Lineker happens to be a good friend of mine. Maybe if we just referred to him as "Father Lineker", we could slip him into the team and . . .'

'Outrageous!' cried Monsignor O'Reilly. 'We'll do it!'

He was unable to attend the match personally on the Saturday, but at five o'clock Father O'Neal telephoned him with the result. 'Bad news, I'm afraid,' he said. 'The rabbis beat us 4—1.'

'What!' said Monsignor O'Reilly. 'Even with "Father Lineker" playing? Who scored for them?'

'Rabbi Gascoigne and Rabbi Beardsley,' said Father O'Neal.

GRAFFITI

Outside the County Ground at Swindon:
SWINDON TOWN ARE MAGIC!
And underneath:
WATCH THEM DISAPPEAR FROM THE SECOND DIVISION!

On the wall of a chapel in Dumbarton, Scotland:
JESUS SAVES!
And underneath:
DUMBARTON SHOULD SIGN HIM FOR GOAL!

On the toilet wall of a Second Division Club:
STOCKTON-ON-TEAS FOR THE CUP!

On a wall in the Republican area of Belfast:
BRITS OUT!
Under which someone had added:
EXCEPT CHARLTON, SATTERS, TOWNSEND, SHEEDY
AND ALDRIDGE.

A famous English footballer had just been transferred for a record sum of money and was being interviewed on television. 'Do you realise,' said the interviewer, 'that the money you will receive as a result of this transfer, together with your income from endorsements, personal appearances, lecturing and so on will mean that you'll have earned more in one year than the Queen gets from the Civil List?'

'Well, I should hope so!' said the footballer. 'I play a damn sight better than she does.'

A man applied to Sheffield Wednesday FC for a job on the administrative staff. 'What we're really looking for here,' said the chairman, 'is what you might call a "chief worrier"! Someone to worry about things like falling attendances, finances, league promotion, violence on the terraces, and so on. For a chap like that we'd be prepared to pay £25,000 a year. Interested?'

'Certainly,' said the applicant. 'But – you'll pardon me for saying this, I hope – where on earth is Sheffield Wednesday going to find that sort of money for a job like this?'

'Ah!' said the chairman. 'That would be your first worry.'

The office-boy had taken the afternoon off to attend his uncle's funeral. His boss, a keen football fan, went the same afternoon to watch a match between Aberdeen and Celtic, and he saw the office-boy among the crowd. 'So this is your uncle's funeral, is it?' he said sarcastically.

'I shouldn't be at all surprised,' said the office-boy. 'He's the referee.'

A Ballymena United fan travelled to Bangor to see his team play the league leaders. He went into a pub for a few quick ones before the match but stayed rather too long and forgot about the game entirely. The match was long over when he left the pub and he caught the bus home and immediately fell asleep. He woke with a start some time later, and glancing out of the window, saw a sign which read BALLYMENA 30, BANGOR 20. 'Hurray!' he shouted. 'I knew we could beat the beggars!'

An amateur team in the West of Ireland played a match against a team from the local monastery. Just before the kick-off the visiting team, all of whom were monks, knelt down solemnly on the pitch, put their hands together and indulged in five minutes of silent prayer. The monastery then proceeded to trounce their hosts 9—0. After the match the home team captain said, 'Well, boys, we've been out-played before but this is the first time we've ever been out-prayed!'

A spectator at a match in the North of England kept up a constant barrage of insults and derogatory remarks directed against the referee. Finally the ref could stand it no longer. He marched over to the stand and, looking the noisy spectator squarely in the eye, shouted, 'Look here – I've been watching you for the last twenty minutes . . .'

'I thought so,' the spectator shouted back. 'I knew you couldn't have been watching the game!'

There was once a fanatical Spurs supporter who thought of nothing but football all day long. He talked about football, read about football, watched nothing but football on television and attended matches as often as he possibly could. At last his poor wife could stand it no longer. One night she said, 'I honestly believe you love Spurs more than you love me!'

'Blimey,' said the fan, 'I love Hartlepool United more than I love you!'

It was only the fourth week of the season and United's new goalkeeper had already let in twenty-seven goals. He was having a drink in a pub one night when a man approached him and said, 'I've been watching you play, son, and I think I might be able to help you.'

'Are you a trainer?' said the young goalkeeper hopefully.

'No,' said the stranger, 'I'm an optician.'

Did you hear what happened to old Andy McTavish last Saturday? He walked all the way to Wembley for the Cup Final to save on the train fare and then had to pay £20 to get in because he was too tired to climb over the wall!

There is only one recorded instance in soccer history of a goalkeeper being struck by lightning during a match. The goalkeeper was killed instantly and went straight to Heaven. He was greeted by an Archangel who offered to show him around. 'Would you like to see our football pitch?' asked the Archangel.

'Football pitch?' said the goalkeeper. 'Do you play football here?'

'Of course,' said the Archangel. 'We're playing Hell tomorrow in the Cup and we needed someone in goal. Why do you think we sent for you?'

Referee: 'Penalty!'
Home captain: 'Who for?'
Referee: 'Us!'

A well-known footballer who was just about to get hitched was holding forth in the local pub. 'It's generally thought,' he said, 'that when a player gets married, he loses his form, but that isn't going to happen to me. No – with Shirley by my side, I shall play better than ever!'

'I've been playing football professionally for ten years now. Of course, my father was dead set against my taking up the game at all. In fact he offered me £5,000 not to train.'

'Really? What did you do with the money?'

Irish football supporter: 'How much is it to come in?'
Ticket clerk: '£6. And that's standing room only.
Irish football supporter: 'Well, here's £3. I've only got one
                        leg.'

The manager of a Fourth Division club called his leading goal-scorer into his office. 'You've played so well this season,' he said, 'that the committee has decided to give you a special bonus. We would like you to accept this cheque for £500.'

'Thank you very much,' said the player. 'That's very kind of you.'

'And,' continued the manager, 'if you play as well for the rest of the season, the chairman will sign it for you.'

A man walked into the office of a large London firm and said to the manager, 'I'm young Cartwright's grandfather – he works in your mail room here. I just popped in to ask if you could give him the afternoon off so I could take him to the League Final at Wembley.'

'I'm afraid he's not here,' said the manager. 'We already gave him the afternoon off to go to your funeral.'

A small boy stopped Derby County's Kevin Francis after a League game and said, 'Could I have your autograph, please?'

'But I gave you my autograph last week, didn't I?' said Kevin.

'Yes, I know,' said the boy. 'But if I can get ten of yours, I can swap them for one of Peter Shilton's.'

A week before the Cup Final at Wembley a few years ago there was an advertisement in *The Times* which read: 'Man offers marriage to woman supplying Cup Final ticket for next Saturday. Replies must enclose photograph of ticket.'

'You're looking worried.'
'Yes. My doctor's just told me I can't play football.'
'Oh! He's seen you play, has he?'

There was trouble on the terraces at The Hawthorns one Saturday afternoon. A huge West Bromwich Albion fan picked up a tiny spectator wearing the blue and white colours of Millwall, the visiting team. As he was about to hurl him to the ground, one of his mates yelled, 'Hey, Derek, don't waste him! Chuck him at the referee!'

A Manchester City fan came down to Wembley for the Cup Final. As he didn't have a ticket he asked a tout outside the gates how much the cheapest one cost. '£25,' said the tout.
'£25!' said the fan. 'Back in Manchester I could get a woman for that!'
'Maybe,' said the tout. 'But you wouldn't get an hour and a half with the Band of the Coldstream Guards in the interval!'

A woman was reading a newspaper one morning and said to her husband, 'Look at this, dear. There's an article here about a man who traded his wife for a season ticket to Arsenal. You wouldn't do a thing like that, would you?'
'Of course I wouldn't!' replied her husband. 'The season's almost over!'

There was once a football match between two small village teams. The visitors were surprised to see that the home team's goalkeeper was a horse. The horse played extremely well and it was mainly due to him that the home team won. After the match the visiting captain said to the home captain, 'How on earth did a horse ever learn to keep goal like that?'

'How does anyone learn?' answered the home captain. 'Practice, practice, practice!'

The shrill blast of the whistle and the pointing finger of the referee stopped the player in his tracks. The referee beckoned him over and produced notebook, pencil and yellow card. 'It's a yellow card for you,' said the referee, waving the card at the footballer.

'You know what you can do with your yellow card!' shouted the player.

'You're too late, mate,' replied the referee. 'There's three red cards there already!'

A visiting fan turned up at a Maidstone—Cardiff match last week and was told that seats were £6, £10 and £15, and programmes £1. 'OK,' he said cheerfully, 'I'll sit on a programme!'

'How did you enjoy your holiday in Israel?'
'Great!'
'Did you visit the Wailing Wall?'
'Yes – but I couldn't get near it for West Ham supporters!'

One of the Southern League's stadiums is several miles out of town, right next to a large farm. During a match one Saturday afternoon the ball was kicked clear out of the ground and landed in the farmyard in the middle of a group of chickens and a rooster. The rooster looked at the ball thoughtfully for a few moments and then said quietly, 'Ladies, I don't want to criticise, but I'd just like you all to take a look at the kind of work that's being turned out on other farms.'

A fellow had arranged to take his girlfriend to a local match but unfortunately they were delayed and didn't arrive until nearly half-time. 'What's the score?' the lad asked a bystander.

'Nil–nil,' was the reply.

'Oh, good!' his girlfriend gushed. 'We haven't missed anything!'

The boss called the office-boy into his private sanctum. 'How did your great-aunt's funeral go yesterday afternoon?' he asked.

'It went off all right, sir,' said the office-boy, puzzled.

'Good, good,' said the boss. 'Pity they've got to do it all over again.'

'Pardon, sir?' said the office-boy.

'Yes. I understand there's a replay on Saturday.'

'What's the best way to contact your long-lost relatives?' 'Win the football pools!'

A goalkeeper in the Second Division had the unfortunate habit of breaking wind when facing a penalty kick, a habit which was very off-putting for the kicker. On one occasion during an important cup match a penalty was awarded against his team. The striker placed the ball carefully, measured his run-up, cleaned the toe of his boot, and kicked. The ball went straight to the goalkeeper, who caught it cleanly without any bother.

'Sorry about that,' said the striker to his captain. 'It was his breaking wind that put me off.'

'But he didn't break wind this time,' replied the captain.

'No, I know,' said the striker. 'But I allowed for it.'

A bishop and a football manager both died on the same day and arrived at the Pearly Gates together. St Peter ignored the bishop but made a great fuss of the manager and welcomed him with open arms. The bishop was understandably puzzled over this and, approaching St Peter, he said, 'I don't want to be presumptuous, but I am a bishop and you haven't spoken a word to me. Yet that football manager is getting a rapturous welcome!'

'Well,' said St Peter, 'we get hundreds of bishops up here but this is the first football manager we've ever had!'

A famous footballer was killed in a car crash. Arriving in Heaven, he was greeted by the angel on duty at the gates. The angel took down the necessary particulars and then said, 'Is there anything you did on earth which would stop you from entering Heaven?'

'Well,' replied the footballer, 'I did once cheat in a very important football match.'

'Oh, dear!' cried the angel. 'Tell me what happened.'

'I was playing for Ireland against England and I scored a goal. I was offside at the time but the referee didn't notice and allowed the goal. As a result we won the match because that was the only goal scored.'

'Am I to understand that your action won the game for Ireland?' asked the angel.

'That is correct – and it's been worrying me for years.'

'Well, you can stop worrying. What you did was fine, so in you go!'

'Well!' said the player, pleasantly surprised. 'Thank you very much, Peter!'

'Oh, I'm not St Peter,' smiled the angel, 'I'm St Patrick!'

An unlucky footballer died and found himself outside the gates of Hell. 'Come in, come in!' said the devil on duty at the gate. 'We've been expecting you. You're Bill Rowlands, the famous footballer, aren't you?'

'That's right,' said Rowlands. 'Tell me, do you have any football pitches down here?'

'Oh yes,' said the devil. 'Dozens of them!'

'Great!' said the footballer. 'Of course, I haven't got any kit. I suppose you'll be able to supply boots and shorts – and, of course, a ball?'

'Boots and shorts, yes,' said the devil with a smile, 'but I'm afraid there are no balls down here.'

'What!' cried the footballer in astonishment. 'Dozens of pitches and not a single ball?'

'That's right,' said the devil. 'That's the hell of it!'

Tommy Docherty, the legendary manager, died and went straight up to Heaven. God said, 'Who are you?' as Docherty strode up to the Celestrial Throne.

'I'm Tommy Docherty,' he said. 'And that's my chair you're sitting in!'

There was once a big football match between Heaven and Hell for the Celestial Cup. An angel was talking to a devil on the night before the match and remarked, 'It should be a walkover for us, you know. We've got all the good footballers up here.'

'Yes, I know,' said the devil with a fiendish grin. 'But we've got all the referees down there!'

All through the match a well-dressed man in the crowd kept up a constant barrage of criticism directed at the referee. He questioned every decision and was scathing in his opinion of the referee's abilities and competence. When the game was over the referee went over to the heckler and asked him if he had a business card.

'Certainly,' said the man, somewhat surprised, and handed over a card on which was printed HENRY ADAMS, SOLICITOR.

'Thanks,' said the referee. 'I'll be in to see you on Monday morning.'

'All right,' said the solicitor. 'Legal problem, is it?'

'Oh, no, nothing like that,' said the referee. 'I'm just coming round to tell you how to run *your* business!'

A man holding a football leaned over his garden gate and shouted to two boys standing on the other side of the street, 'Is this your ball?'

'Did it do any damage, mister?' asked one of the lads.

'No, it didn't.'

'Then it's ours,' said the boy.

One boy asked another, 'Did I bring you back that football I borrowed last week?'

'No, you didn't,' said his pal.

'Damn!' said the first lad. 'I wanted to borrow it again!'

Two keen fans at a local derby were so engrossed in the match that, although they were both starving, they didn't want to take time out to go across to the refreshment stand. They noticed a young lad nearby and said, 'Here, kid, here's £1.50 – nip over there and get us a couple of hot-dogs, and one for yourself.'

A few minutes later the kid returned, chewing on a hot-dog, and handed them £1. 'Here's your change,' he said. 'They only had one hot-dog left.'

A small boy got lost at a football match. He went up to a policeman and said, 'I've lost my dad!'

The policeman said, 'What's he like?'

To which the little boy replied, 'Beer and women!'

At a school football match the goalkeeper collided with the goalpost and fell to the ground. Several boys gathered around him but, as his recovery appeared to be taking some time, the sportsmaster ran over to the group. 'What's the matter?' he asked.

'We're trying to give him the kiss of life, sir,' said one of the boys, 'but he keeps getting up and walking away!'

Two boys were playing football in the back garden with a new football.

'Where did you get that ball?' asked their mother.

'We found it.'

'Are you sure it was lost?'

'Oh, yes. We saw them looking for it.'

At a World Cup game between England and West Germany, the referee was a Brazilian who spoke very little English. He had occasion to warn one of the England players for tripping. When this happened a second time the Brazilian referee said angrily, 'You trip again! Now is no more tripping or is yellow card for you!' Ten minutes later the English player committed yet another blatant foul.

The referee rushed up in a rage and, as he approached, the English player said, 'Oh bugger off!'

The referee said, 'All right! As you have apologise, no card this time. But next time – off!'

A shipwrecked sailor found himself on a remote island in the Pacific. The only other inhabitant appeared to be a very beautiful native girl. On the first day she fed him with delicious native foods. On the second day she gave him lovely cooling drinks. On the third day, to the sailor's surprise, she produced a carton of cigarettes. By this time the sailor was beginning to enjoy life on the island. On the fourth day the girl smiled at him seductively and asked, 'Would you like to play a game?'

'Blimey!' said the sailor. 'Don't tell me you've got a football pitch on the island as well!'

There was once a famous football star who rather fancied himself as God's gift to the ladies. He fell in love with a local girl and approached her father to ask for permission to marry her.

'My daughter marry a football player?' shouted the father. 'Over my dead body!'

'But, sir, you haven't even seen me play!' protested the star.

'Well, all right, then – I'll come to the match on Saturday.'

After the match the father came into the dressing rooms and shook the footballer warmly by the hand. 'Of course you can marry my daughter, my boy! You're no more a football player than I am!'

After the season was over a couple of the players used their savings to go on safari in Africa. The highlight of their trip was seeing a lion in his natural habitat after making a kill. Suddenly the lion began to walk purposefully towards them. One of the players immediately began to put on a pair of jogging shoes. His friend said, 'You're wasting your time! You'll never outrun that lion!'

'Maybe not,' said his friend, 'but if I can outrun you, I'll be laughing!'

Milligan went to see his home team play one Saturday afternoon and lost £20 betting on the home side. After dinner that evening he went to the pub where the match was being shown on television. 'I'll bet any man here £20 the home side wins!' he roared.

Several of the regulars took him up on the bet with the result that he lost a small fortune. When he got home he told his wife what had happened.

'You great idiot!' she shouted. 'Why did you bet on a home

win when you'd seen the home team get beat this afternoon?'

'Well,' said Milligan, 'I didn't think they'd make the same mistakes twice!'

A woman wanted to go to a football match with her husband, who was a keen follower of the game, so he agreed to take her to the next available match. It took her some time to decide what to wear and they arrived just in time for the kick-off. Her husband was soon shouting and yelling with the rest of the crowd, but it was obvious she hadn't a clue what it was all about.

'Look, darling,' her husband explained slowly, 'the object of the game is to get the ball into one or other of the nets at each end of the field.'

'Wouldn't it be easier,' said his wife, 'if they didn't get in each other's way so much?'

'Who's this Bill Baker everyone's talking about?'

'You mean to say you don't know? He's the bloke that saved United from relegation last Saturday.'

'What position does he play?'

'Position? He doesn't play – he was the referee.'

It was a needle match between Celtic and Rangers at Glasgow's Ibrox Park. A mild little man was accosted by a huge and aggressive supporter in full regalia. 'Are ye a Celtic fan or a Rangers fan?' he growled menacingly.

'Neither, really,' said the little man nervously. 'I just like watching football.'

'Och,' snarled the Scot, 'a bloody atheist, eh?'

Joe was admiring a silver cup in a display cabinet. It was inscribed TO THE FOOTBALLER OF THE YEAR. 'Hey, Mickey,' he said, 'I didn't know you were interested in football.'

'I'm not,' said Mickey.

'But you've got a silver cup inscribed to the footballer of the year in your cabinet.'

'Oh, I got that for running.'

'Running?' said Joe. 'How the hell did you get a football cup for running?'

'Simple,' said Mickey. 'When no one was looking, I grabbed it and ran.'

A certain Fourth Division club was right at the bottom of the ladder so the coach instituted a course of retraining for the coming season. As many of the team members seemed to be ignorant of the basics of the game, he decided to start at the beginning. He picked up a ball and said, 'Now, gentlemen, the object I'm holding is called a football. Now the object of the game is . . .'

From the back came an agitated voice: 'Hang on a minute, coach! Not so fast!'

A football widow was complaining to her husband that his passion for the game was ruining their marriage. 'You never take me out,' she wailed. 'You never buy me presents. You're never at home if there's a match on anywhere. You never even remember our anniversary. Why I'll bet you've even forgotten the date of our wedding!'

'Of course I haven't!' scoffed her husband. 'It was the day Sweden beat Germany in the UEFA Under-Eighteen Championship at Lomma!'

Another Elephants United match that has gone down in the annals of soccer history is the one they played against a team composed entirely of ants – Ants Athletic. Shortly before half-time, one of the Elephant defenders stepped on the Ants' striker and squashed him flat. 'Sorry about that, ref,' he said apologetically, 'I only meant to trip him.'

A player was taken to hospital with a dislocated knee, incurred during a match, and his agonised roarings were heard all over casualty as the doctor tried to put the joint back into place. Said the doctor, 'For a supposedly hardened League player, you're making a hell of a lot of fuss. There's a woman next door who's having a baby and she isn't making half the fuss you're making!'

'Maybe so,' said the injured player. 'But in her case, nobody's trying to push anything back in!'

'I played in a match last week with Maradona!'
'You didn't!'
'Yes, I did. He said to me, "If you're a footballer I'm Maradona!"'

A talent scout for a First Division team was touring Ireland. He attended a local match between two small town teams and was amazed by the skill of one of the players. He approached the player after the match and offered him a place in the First Division team, with a very attractive salary. 'We'd like to have you,' he said, 'and if there's anything you want, or any special requests, you only have to ask.'

'Well,' said the local man, 'I would like to join your team but there is one condition.'

'What is it?'

'I'd like to have Saturday afternoons off to play for my old team.'

No collection of football anecdotes would be complete without mention of the legendary Elephants United team. On one occasion the Elephants (playing at their home ground Pachyderm Park, in their usual colours – grey trunks) were matched against a team of Insects. By half-time in this somewhat one-sided match, the Elephants were leading by 149 goals to nil. At the start of the second half, however, the Insects sent in a new forward, a centipede. Immediately the game changed and the Insects took command of the match. The centipede scored again and again, and proved to be completely unstoppable. The final score was 703 goals to 150 in the Insects' favour.

After the match the Elephant captain said to his opposite number, a water-beetle, 'That centipede of yours was great! I can't understand why you didn't use him from the start.'

'We would have done, believe me,' said the Insect captain, 'but it takes him forty-five minutes to get his boots on.'

'Shoot, Gazza, shoot!' yelled a fan at a crucial moment in England's World Cup match against Italy.

'Shoot Gazza!' said his disgruntled neighbour. 'I wish they'd shoot the whole ruddy lot of them!'

A group of supporters of the local football team assembled outside the gates just before kick-off and discovered that one member was missing. 'Oh, yes, I remember,' said one of them. 'Harry said something about getting married this afternoon at two-thirty.'

'You must be joking!' said his neighbour. 'That means he won't get here until half-time!'

The home captain was talking to the visiting referee. 'Now we don't expect any favouritism,' he said. 'However, I'd like to point out that our ground is next to a hospital and there's a canal over on the far side – and we haven't lost a home match all season.'

A bald-headed goalkeeper jumped frantically at an incoming ball and headed it into his own goal. 'Oi, mate!' shouted a voice from the crowd. 'You forgot to chalk yer cue!'

A Fourth Division goalkeeper missed a simple kick at goal and as he picked up the ball from the back of the net, a spectator shouted, 'Call yourself a goalkeeper? I could have caught that shot in me mouth!'

'So could I,' the goalkeeper yelled back, 'if my mouth was as big as yours!'

A Fourth Division team was about to play the First Division leaders in a Cup match, and the manager was giving them a last-minute pep-talk. 'All right, lads,' he said. 'Go out there and slay them! You'll be the giant-killers of the decade. And then I'll get enough money to replace the lot of you!'

One Saturday morning a man was standing at the bar staring thoughtfully into his pint of beer. A friend approached and asked, 'What's bothering you, Joe? You're really deep in thought.'

'Well,' said Joe, 'this morning my wife ran away with my best friend.'

'Joe!' said his friend sympathetically. 'That's terrible!'

'It certainly is,' agreed Joe. 'It means we're short of a goalkeeper for the match this afternoon.'

England was playing Ireland and the ground was packed. There wasn't an empty seat – except for the one next to Mike Murphy. Mike's friend, Pat, tapped him on the shoulder and said, 'How come you have an empty seat beside you?'

'Oh, that was for the wife,' said Mike.

'Didn't she want to come to the match?'

'It's not that. You see, she died three days ago.'

'Oh, I am sorry,' said Pat. 'Couldn't one of your friends have come instead so as not to waste the seat?'

'Not really,' answered Mike. 'They all wanted to go to the funeral.'

Little Jimmy came home from school one day and let himself into the house. Everything was quiet and he tiptoed to his room. As he passed his mother's door he saw her sitting at the dressing table, hugging herself and moaning, 'I want a man! I want a man!' Jimmy was puzzled but went off to his room without disturbing her. Next day the same thing happened. Again he saw his mother hugging herself and moaning, 'I want a man! I want a man!' The third day, when Jimmy came past his mother's room, she was lying on the bed with a strange man. Quick as a flash, Jimmy ran to his room, sat down in front of the mirror and started chanting, 'I want a pair of football boots! I want a pair of football boots!'

A forward had a reputation for very hard play and following a match one day he returned to the dressing room with a hell of a leg on him: lacerations down the shin-bone, dislocated knee cap, bruising to the thigh and grazes everywhere. The only trouble was he didn't know who the leg belonged to.

The championship team had been playing away, and after the match the bus they were travelling home in was involved in a serious accident. The driver, the manager, and all the players were killed instantly. The only survivor was the team mascot – a chimpanzee. Soon after the disaster, investigators came out to determine the cause of the accident. They interviewed the chimp, who gave all his answers in sign language.

'Just before the crash, what was the driver doing?'

The chimp made signs to indicate drinking and smoking.

'And what was the manager doing?'

More signs of drinking and smoking.

'And the rest of the team?'

Actions of drinking and smoking and general carrying-on.

'This is terrible!' said one of the investigators. 'They must have been having some kind of party on the bus!' Then, turning to the chimp, he asked, 'What were *you* doing just before the crash?'

Whereupon the chimp went through the motions of driving a bus.

Boss: 'You told me you were going to see your dentist yesterday, but I saw you at White Hart Lane with a friend.

Employee: 'That's right, sir – that was my dentist.'

The goalkeeper wasn't looking at all happy and a friend said, 'I hear you didn't do so well in goal this afternoon.'

'Listen,' said the goalkeeper. 'If I hadn't been there, we'd have lost 25—nil!'

'Oh? What was the final score then?'

'24—nil!'

As the funeral procession passed along the street a passer-by noticed a pair of football boots on the coffin which was being carried by four young men. He nudged the man standing next to him and, pointing to the boots, said, 'Well-known footballer, was he?'

'Oh, no,' came the reply. 'Those belong to one of the bearers. He kicks off at two-thirty.'

On the day Aldershot lost 10—1 at Southend in the Leyland Daf Cup, Len Walker, the Aldershot manager, was seen walking through the town with a video recorder under his arm. 'What's the recorder for, Len?' asked a passing fan.

'I got it for the team,' said the beleaguered manager.

'Reckon you got a damned good bargain then,' said the disgruntled supporter.

It is recorded with great authority that, in the days when players received a maximum wage and also different rates for the winter and summer periods, the legendary Tom Finney left the manager's office, having negotiated the coming season. 'What did you get, Tom?' asked his team-mate, waiting his turn.

'£12 a week, winter and summer,' replied the Peerless Plumber.

The team-mate took his place in the manager's office. 'Now then, lad,' said the manager, 'you've not done bad, so I'm giving you a new contract. You'll get £12 a week in the winter and £8 in the summer.'

'But, gaffer,' protested the player, 'Finney's getting £12 a week all year!'

'Yes, son,' frowned the manager, 'but he's a better player than you.'

'Not in the summer, he's not!' was the explosive retort.

A team manager came home unexpectedly one evening when a game he was due to watch was called off. He found the house in darkness, slipped in quietly, mounted the stairs and switched on the bedroom light to discover his assistant in bed with his wife. 'Tommy!' he said sadly. 'I *have* to. But you?'

Two small boys wearing T-shirts were spotted on the beach at Southend. One shirt carried the legend LABOUR WINS SOUTHEND EAST! The other boy's T-shirt read: SOUTHEND UNITED WIN EUROPEAN CUP! The two lads went into the sea for a swim and swam quite a way out. Suddenly the onlookers saw to their horror the dreaded triangular fin of a shark accelerating towards the boys through the water. The watchers could only stand there as first one boy and then the other disappeared under the waves. But after a couple of minutes one of the boys reappeared and made his way, ashore.

He was helped out of the water by the former MP for Southend, Teddy Taylor. As Teddy lifted the boy up he noticed that the survivor wore the shirt bearing the legend: SOUTHEND UNITED WIN EUROPEAN CUP! 'Are you all right?' he said solicitously. 'How was it that the shark ate your friend but let you go?'

The boy pointed to his T-shirt. 'No problem, Mr Taylor,' he said. 'Not even a shark could swallow this!'

It is the custom for vociferous football supporters to chant the name of their team, letter by letter. Thus Tottenham Hotspur fans will shout, 'Give us an S, give us a P, give us a U . . .' and so on. Brian Naysmith, Fulham's chief executive, suggests that the most hated German football fan is the one who stands on the terraces of Borussia Mönchengladbach and shouts, 'Give us a B, give us an O, give us an R . . .!'

There's a little grocer's shop just around the corner from London's Connaught Rooms, and one morning a man walked in and bought up all the rotten eggs, old tomatoes and cabbages on the shelves. The assistant grinned. 'I bet you're going to that talk Brian Clough's giving tonight at the Connaught Rooms, about the England World Cup team!'

'No,' said the stranger. 'I *am* Brian Clough!'

There was once a manager of a small and unsuccessful Fourth Division club who had a rather inflated notion of his own prowess and leadership. He attended a convention of club managers at the Savoy Hotel and fell into conversation with a well-known sports commentator. Looking round at the assembled team bosses, he remarked, 'How many great club managers do you think there are in this room?'

'One less than you think!' replied the commentator.

A team manager was once having a drink in a pub when a horse walked in and ordered a pint of lager. They fell into conversation and the horse revealed that he was himself a keen player. 'Is there a chance of getting a trial for your club?' he asked.

'What position do you play?' asked the manager.

'Goalkeeper,' replied the horse.

The manager, who had a nose for talent, invited the horse to turn out for the team on the following Saturday. The horse accepted. For four consecutive Saturdays the horse played for the team and not once did the ball pass him. He was superb! After the fourth game the manager said, 'You're playing brilliantly in goal, but as we're not scoring any ourselves, I'm thinking of pushing you up the field and making you a striker.'

'But that would mean I'd have to run!' protested the horse.

'Of course you'd have to run!' said the manager.

'But I can't run!' said the horse. 'If I could run, I'd be at Ascot instead of here playing this bloody stupid game!'

During the 1920s there was a certain Lord Kinnaird who, in his youth had been a keen footballer. He used to tell the story of a match in which he took part: an opposing forward made a very tricky run and Kinnaird went to tackle him, feeling quite confident of getting the ball away from him. But as he approached, the opposing forward said, 'Let me score! I want to get my name in the papers!'

'He did score, too,' said Lord Kinnaird, 'for I was so tickled that I couldn't do a thing! He easily dribbled round me, and shot straight into the net!'

Two rival football managers, Connors and Hargreaves, were continually trying to outdo each other. Whatever improvements Connors introduced into his club, Hargreaves had to go one better. When Connors had floodlights installed, Hargreaves had a new stand built. When Connors ordered new luxury coaches to transport the team to away matches, Hargreaves installed closed-circuit television. Then Connors bought a vintage Bentley worth £30,000. Shortly afterwards, Hargreaves acquired a white Rolls-Royce with a built-in bar. Connors countered by having a car-phone installed in his Bentley and immediately Hargreaves did the same. To show that he was keeping up with his rival, Hargreaves made a call from his Rolls-Royce to Connors' Bentley. Connors' chauffeur answered the call. 'I'd like to speak to Mr Connors, please,' said Hargreaves smugly.

'I'm sorry, sir,' said the chauffeur. 'Mr Connors is taking a call on the other line.'

There was once a famous football coach who was notorious for his shortsightedness and for his bad temper. He was conducting a training session on one occasion and noticed that the players were somewhat listless and inattentive. Losing his temper, he shouted, '*You* at the back of the room! What should the full-back do if he's playing on the right and there's a break through on the opposite side of the field?'

'I don't know,' said the chap at the back.

'Well, then, can you tell me the rules governing the defence position when a penalty is being taken?'

'I don't know.'

'I taught you that only yesterday!' bellowed the coach. 'Didn't you hear what I said?'

'I wasn't here,' said the man.

'Where were you then?'

'I was having a few drinks with some friends.'

The coach turned purple. 'You have the audacity to tell me that! How do you expect to improve?'

'I don't, coach. I'm an electrician and I just came in here to fix the lights.'

A disgraceful brawl took place at a recent Southern League match and on the following Wednesday evening a tribunal met to determine the cause of the incident. They called in the captain of the home team and said, 'Will you tell the tribunal in your own words how the fight started.'

'I didn't see any fight,' said the captain.

'You didn't? Well then tell us what you did see.'

'Well,' said the captain, 'Parker elbowed Thomas in the stomach, and as he went down, he put his hand in the mud and Bannerman stood on it. Then Parker's mate, Gibson, punched Bannerman in the mouth and knocked out a couple of teeth. Thomas got up and flattened Parker, and I could see the whole thing was probably going to turn into a fight, so I left the pitch.'

The village football team found itself short of a goalkeeper at an important match one Saturday afternoon. Rather than play a man short, the captain asked a young man who was standing on the touchline if he would go into goal.

'Oh, I don't know anything about the game,' said the man.

'That's all right,' said the captain. 'All you have to do is make sure the ball doesn't go between the posts.'

Reluctantly, the young man agreed to play, and by half-time he had let in eight goals without making any attempt to stop them.

'You might at least try to stop the ball!' said the captain. 'I did explain what you had to do!'

'Yes, I know what you said,' replied the young man 'but I don't see why I should throw myself all over the place to try and stop the ball when there's a perfectly good net there for that very purpose!'

For the third time in the first ten minutes of the match the referee awarded a penalty against the home team. An angry supporter shouted, 'Oi, ref, are you blind or what?'

The referee strode over to the touchline and demanded, 'What was that you said?'

'Blimey' the fan shouted back, 'Are you deaf as well?'

'Was there a big crowd at the match on Saturday?'

'Big crowd? There were so few of us, the players gave us a round of applause when we walked in!'

I went to Highbury last Saturday and I've never seen so many people trying to get into a match! I said to the fellow next to me, 'Do you think we'll get in?'

He said, 'I hope so! I'm the referee!'

A former footballer who had become rather corpulent was asked to turn out for a charity match but he refused. 'I'm so disappointed!' said the organiser. 'Won't you change your mind?'

'No, son, I won't,' said the ex-footballer. 'I tried it a few years ago. As soon as the ball came towards me, my brain rapped out all the old commands – run towards the ball at speed, trap it, beat the defender, kick for goal . . . !'

'So it's all still there, then!' said the organiser.

'No, it isn't. You see, when my brain rapped out the orders, my body said, "Who me?" '

A new amateur team had just been formed in a northern mining town. Just before their first match the team captain addressed the lads. 'Now remember, boys,' he said, 'if you don't have possession, go for their shins or their ankles. Trip 'em up, and when they're down, make sure they stay down. Now then – who's got the ball?

'Never mind the ball,' said a voice from the back. 'Let's get on with the bloody game!'

A television programme called 'Great Sportsmen of the Past' was being prepared recently and a researcher was sent to interview a former footballer now in his nineties. The fellow had done his preliminary research and knew he was in the presence of one of the all-time greats of football. His skill on the field had been unequalled, his sportsmanship renowned. After a very interesting interview the researcher said, 'One last question, sir. In your long and outstanding career as a footballer, is there anything you would change if you had to do it all over again?'

The old footballer pondered for a moment and then answered, 'Yes. I'd probably let my moustache grow longer.'

A centipede applied for a trial with a football team and was being interviewed by the coach. 'What position do you play?' asked the coach.

'I'm a striker,' said the centipede.

'Interesting,' said the coach. 'Which is your kicking foot?'

'I can kick with my left or my right,' said the centipede, 'but my best foot is my right, my right, my right, my right, my right, my right . . .'

'My brother's got dozens of trophies and medals for football.'

'Does he play for England?'

'He doesn't play at all. He owns a pawnshop.'

The local beauty queen was the guest of honour at a celebration given by a football team which had just won the Southern League championship. In her speech she pointed out that the life of a beauty queen was very similar to that of a footballer. 'In fact,' she said, 'I've probably worked out more defences against passes than any of you here tonight!'

'I hear your team took your 21—0 defeat last Saturday very badly.'

'Yes, they did.'

'Sad about the goalkeeper. Could some of the players not have stopped him hanging himself from the goalposts?'

'Stopped him! Who the hell do you think helped him tie the rope to the crossbar?'

Two men were sitting in a pub watching 'Match of the Day' on television. It was a First Division game and one of the men remarked, 'You know, the manager of the home team was trying to get me for months.'

'Was he?' said his friend. 'Who were you playing with at the time?'

'His wife!'

'Do you know,' asked the vicar, 'what happens to little boys who play football every Sunday afternoon instead of coming to Bible class?'

'Yes,' replied little Sammy. 'They grow up to play in the First Division, become international stars, appear on television, and get very, very rich!'

The Cup Final was being shown on television and a viewer was yelling and shouting as loudly as the fans at the ground. 'I can't understand what all the fuss is about,' said his wife as she handed him a cup of tea. 'I thought they decided who the champions were last year!'

'I hear your football club is looking for a treasurer.'

'That's right.'

'But didn't you take on a new treasurer last month?'

'Yes – that's the one we're looking for!'

The girls in the factory had accepted a challenge football match with the men. They insisted on having a training session first and the men agreed that they would leave the ground and let the girls practise unobserved. On the evening in question, the men finished their training session and, as arranged left the field. The girls went out onto the field, selected two teams and were just about to start when they realised they hadn't got a ball. One of the girls was sent to the pavilion to get one but returned empty-handed. 'All the men have gone home,' she wailed, 'and taken their balls with them!'

A man had a son in the local team and never missed a match. However, one Saturday afternoon the team had an away match and he was unable to attend the game. He asked his son to telephone the result as soon as the game was over. When the call came through his wife picked up the telephone and after listening for a few moments, reported, 'It's Tom – he says he's had his nose broken, some teeth knocked out, and he's lost an ear!'

'Yes, yes,' said the father impatiently. 'But who won?'

The coach was tearing a strip off his star centre-half. 'Your game's gone all to hell,' he said, 'and I know the reason why. You're meant to be in training. See that you stay away from women until the end of the season! I don't want to hear about you taking a girl out again. Is that clear?'

'OK, OK,' said the player. 'No more dates until the end of the season.'

However, the next day the coach was walking down the street when who should he bump into but the same player with a voluptuous blonde on his arm.

'Now look,' said the player. 'Don't get excited! This lady is my wife.'

'*Your* wife!' roared the coach. 'Why, you bastard – that's *my* wife!'

At the end of every football season, every keen football fan has to go through the same ritual:

1. Relearn the names of all his children.
2. Replace the springs in the sofa.
3. Sign up his wife for a course in remedial sex.

There was a report last week that a British underwear company brought out a new brassiere to coincide with the 1990 World Cup. They called it 'Scotland' – it had plenty of support but no cups.

Overheard in the boardroom: 'He's definitely an honest referee. When he's bought, he stays bought.'

One of the senior members of the football club was attending a club dinner. About halfway through he telephoned his wife. 'You know, my dear,' he said, 'there's something very unexpected here. I thought it would be just drinking and speeches, but there are naked girls dancing on the tables, and they're going under the tables with the men. What do you think I should do?'

'If you think you can do anything,' said the wife, 'come home immediately!'

A chap somewhat the worse for liquor staggered up to the turnstiles at a Wigan home match last Saturday. 'I'm not selling you a ticket,' said the attendant. 'You're drunk!'

'Of course I'm drunk!' said the man. 'You don't think I'd come to a Wigan match sober, do you?'

'I hear you've got a new job?'

'That's right. It's one of the easiest jobs I've ever had.'

'What do you do?'

'I keep score for Stockport County.'

At a recent match between Everton and Liverpool a huge supporter wearing the home team's blue and white colours suddenly turned to a meek little man in Liverpool's reds and punched him on the nose.

'Was that meant as a joke?' said the little man.

'No, it wasn't!' bellowed the six-footer.

'That's all right, then,' said the little Liverpool supporter. 'I don't like jokes like that.'

Reporter: 'Congratulations on your big pools win! £200,000! That's quite a tidy sum. What are you going to do with it all?'

Pools winner: 'I'm going to take a cruise round the world, staying in all the best hotels – that'll cost me about £50,000. Then I'll spend £50,000 on the horses and cards, £30,000 on women, and £20,000 on boozing it up.'

Reporter: 'And what about the remaining £50,000?'

Pools winner: 'Oh, I'll probably just blow that!'

A businessman came home one evening in a thoroughly bad mood. His wife asked him, 'What's got into you?'

'One of the juniors asked for the afternoon off to go to his grandmother's funeral. I thought it was the old trick to get to the football game, so I followed him.'

'Was it a good game?' asked the wife.

'Game be damned! It *was* his grandmother's funeral!'

Mother: 'Well, how did you like your visit to the British Museum with Daddy?'

Billy: 'Great! Our team won 5—3!'

It had been a bad day for the club's leading striker. Six times goals had been set up for him, and six times he had missed. As he entered the dressing room, he asked, 'Has anyone got 10p? I want to telephone a friend.'

'Here's 20p,' said the captain. 'Telephone all your friends!'

A footballer broke his leg in a home match one Saturday afternoon and had to go to hospital. A few days later one of the other players visited him. The injured footballer was by no means the team's best player, and was rather worried about losing his place on the team.

'Oh, you don't want to worry about that,' said his fellow-player. 'Why, everyone's been talking about you. Only yesterday, the captain said, "Whatever happened to old what's-his-name?"'

A couple of fans turned up recently at Doncaster's Belle Vue ground, handed over £20 and said, 'Two, please.'

'Right,' said the ticket clerk. 'What would you like – strikers, wing-halves, full-backs . . . ?'

Punter: '£50 on Liverpool to beat Dundee.'
Bookie: 'Sorry – we don't take bets on friendlies.'
Punter: 'Don't be daft! Liverpool don't play friendlies!'

'What happens exactly at a football match?'

'Well, two teams of eleven players each go on to a large field and they try to kick a ball into a net while another person, called a referee, watches them.'

'What happens when the referee isn't watching them?'

'Well, then they kick each other.'

A famous football coach was finishing his pep-talk to the team just before an important match. 'Remember, men,' he said, 'football builds leadership, initiative and individuality! Now get out on to that field and do exactly as I've told you!'

Woody had played like a hairy goat all afternoon. When the team came off the ground after the final whistle, he said sheepishly to the coach, 'Sorry about that. I'm not playing my usual game today.'

'What game is that then?' said the coach. 'Croquet?'

An Irish team was visiting Spain on an international tour. Their first evening was free and one player went to another hotel to have a drink. He was sitting at the bar when an attractive Spanish girl came up and sat on the stool next to him. 'Hello,' said the player. 'Do you speak English?'

'Jos a leetle bit,' she smiled.

'How much?' asked the footballer.

'£25,' said the girl seductively.

'What happened at the game today?' asked Billy.

'That bloody referee was playing for the other side,' answered Andy. 'Three of our fellows got fouled. Smith got an elbow in the eye, Martin got a kick on the knee, and Hoffman got a knee in the crutch! And all the referee could say was that he wasn't in the right position to see the fouls!'

'Wasn't he in position to see anything?'

'Only when Smith punched him on the nose – he was perfectly positioned for that!'

There was a report in the paper last week about a young man who won £250,000 on the football pools. Apparently he had told his mother and father that he was generously going to give them £50 each out of his winnings. The old couple were so upset that the father confessed that they were not the young man's real parents. 'What!' he yelled. 'Are you telling me that I'm a bastard?'

'You are that,' said his father. 'And a damn mean one at that!'

'That new centre-forward is a steady player, isn't he.'

'Steady? If he was any steadier, he'd be motionless.'

Tall spectator at football match: 'What a crowd! Why, there must be 30,000 people watching the game this afternoon!'

Small spectator standing behind him: 'Well, let's just say 29,999!'

A policeman on duty at a football ground saw a man with a gorilla walking towards him. He approached the man and said, 'Didn't I speak to you yesterday about that gorilla?'

'That's right, officer,' said the man. 'I found him wandering in the streets and I asked you what I should do with him.'

'And I told you to take it to the zoo.'

'Yes, you did, and I took him to the zoo and he enjoyed it so much, today I thought I'd bring him to a football match!'

A soccer fan has been defined as someone sitting several hundred feet from the ball who can see it better than the referee standing right next to it.

A team manager was talking to a young man who wanted to become a professional footballer. 'You must understand,' he said, 'that if you want to be a really good footballer, the best thing is to give up smoking, drinking and girls.'

'I see,' said the young man thoughtfully. 'Tell me, what's the next best thing?'

Two fans were standing together in the pouring rain, watching the slowest game they had seen all season.

'Tell me again about all the fun we're having,' said one. 'I keep forgetting.'

Did you hear about the Scotsman who sued a Scottish League club because he was injured while watching a match? He fell out of the tree.

First Irishman: 'There's a girl at work who's so stupid, she thinks a football coach has four wheels!'
Second Irishman: 'Would you believe that! How many wheels does it have?'

First wife: 'I find football very educational.'
Second wife: 'How is that?'
First wife: 'Every time my husband turns on the television to watch football, I go into another room and read a book.'

Did you hear about the amateur footballer who was caught accepting payments for matches? He lost his amateur standing so he turned professional and now he's broke.

First girl: 'I hear your Joe's joined United. What position does he play?'
Second girl: 'I'm not sure but I heard some of the other players say he was their main drawback.'

Coach: 'Do you know why you don't score more goals?'
Striker: 'I just can't think.'
Coach: 'That's right!'

A man lay in bed suffering from shock after checking his football coupon to find he had the only eight draws on the Treble Chance and had won £750,000. The doctor examined him and then came downstairs and said to his wife, 'I think he's all right now. He's over the worst of the shock.'

'Oh, good,' said the wife. 'Do you think it's safe to tell him I forgot to post his coupon?'

A fan took his girlfriend to a game for the first time. She couldn't understand what was going on at all and had no idea about the functions of each player. 'What's that man doing standing at the big net?' she asked.

'He's the goalkeeper,' said her boyfriend. 'He has to make sure that the ball doesn't go into the net.'

'And how much does he get for that?'

'Oh, I don't know – about £20,000 a year.'

'Good gracious,' said the young lady. 'Wouldn't it be cheaper to have it boarded up?'

The goalkeeper fancied himself as the star of the team and was very free with his advice to the captain. One Saturday afternoon, as the teams went on to the field he said to the captain. 'You know, you've picked two men this afternoon who should never be in the team at all.'

'Really?' said the captain. 'Who's the other one?'

The referee rushed over to where the player was writhing on the ground just outside the penalty area. 'Did you see who it was that hit you?' he asked.

'No,' groaned the player. 'But I got a note of his number.'

Two Greek immigrants were watching their very first football game. After a few minutes of mystified silence, one turned to the other and said, 'You know, this is all English to me!'

Did you read about that First Division footballer who retired last week with £750,000 in the bank? He claimed that it was due to hard work, perseverance, dedication to the game, and the fact that his uncle died last month and left him £745,000.

Striker: 'Sorry about missing that last goal, chief. I know it was an easy one, and believe me, I could kick myself.'
Coach: 'I shouldn't bother. You'd probably miss.'

'Aren't you going to the Bradford City match this Saturday?'

'Why the hell should I? They didn't come to see me when I was bad!'

After a disastrous game the coach got stuck into one of the worst offenders. 'Fosdyke, you're playing like an old woman! You should be ashamed of yourself! You're useless – a liability to the team!'

After the coach had left, one of Fosdyke's mates tried to console him. 'Don't take any notice of the coach,' he said comfortingly. 'He only repeats what he hears everyone else saying.'

A young Crystal Palace defender had been playing badly all season. Deciding it was time to pull his socks up, he went out one Saturday afternoon and gave it all he'd got. Proud of his efforts, he sought out the coach after the game and asked, 'Well, coach have you noticed any improvement in me since last week?'

The coach looked at him for a moment and then said, 'You've had a haircut!'

The road to Wembley stadium was crowded with fans making their way to the Cup Final. Suddenly a funeral procession passed by, and one fan reverently removed his cap.

'That was a nice gesture,' said his mate.

'It was the least I could do,' said the fan. 'She was a good wife to me for thirty years.'

An ex-player was holding forth in his local to a group of hangers-on. 'When I was playing professionally,' he said, 'I helped Manchester United beat Leeds for three seasons running.'

'Really?' said one listener. 'Which side were you playing for?'

New player: 'Sorry about this afternoon, skipper. I've never played this badly before.'

Captain: 'Oh, you have played before, have you?'

The dressing room had an air of gloom and despondency about it as the captain breezed in to give his players a pep-talk. 'All right, lads,' he said cheerfully, 'this is not the time to be superstitious. Just because we've lost the last twelve games doesn't necessarily mean we're going to lose today!'

Slowly the spectator took off his hat and examined it closely. 'I don't believe it!' he exclaimed. 'There are 30,000 spectators in this ground, plus twenty-two players, two linesmen, one referee and the Band of the Welsh Guards – and that damned pigeon has to pick on me!'

'What's this I hear about your not playing for United any more?'

'That's right.'

'Why's that then?'

'It's all down to something the manager said to me.'

'What did he say?'

'You're fired!'

The referee had just awarded a penalty against the visting team. The player who had committed the foul shouted, 'You're the worst ref I ever saw! I think you stink!'

Picking up the ball, the referee walked back a further fifteen yards from the goal. Then he shouted across to the offending player, 'How do I smell from here?'

A keen player left home to take part in a match one Saturday afternoon, only to return an hour later looking very despondent. 'What's the matter, dear?' asked his wife. 'Was the match cancelled?'

'No. I've been dropped from the team,' replied her husband.

'That's terrible! Did they tell you why?'

'Well, all the captain said was that they didn't allow visitors in the dressing room!'

A small local football team had a run of bad luck and had not scored a single goal in six games. The coach called a training session one Saturday morning and said, 'You all seem to have forgotten how to kick! Now just watch me and see if you can learn something.' He placed the ball twenty yards from the goal and kicked. His shot missed the goal completely. He tried a dozen more kicks and every one of them missed the net. Finally he turned to the team and panted, 'That's the sort of thing you lot have been doing! Now let's see if you can't get out there this afternoon and score some goals!'

Two chaps were walking through a cemetery when they saw a tombstone which bore the legend: HERE LIES A FOOTBALL MANAGER AND AN HONEST MAN. One chap turned to the other and said, 'I didn't know they were allowed to bury two fellows in the same grave.'

A fellow turned up at a match last Saturday just before half-time. He said to a young lady sitting next to him, 'Whose game?'

'I am,' she said sweetly.

A teacher in a London comprehensive asked her class to write a short account of a football match. After a couple of minutes one small boy put down his pen. 'You can't have finished already, Billy,' said the teacher in surprise.

'Yes, I have, miss,' said Billy.

'Well, show me what you've written,' said the teacher.

Billy handed over his work. It consisted of just six words: 'Game cancelled on account of rain.'

'What sort of a match was it last Saturday?'

'Terrible! The only people who played well were the band at half-time.'

MacTavish: 'I hear you went over to Aberdeen to see the match last Saturday, Sandy. Was it a big gate?'

MacDonald: 'It was that, Jock! One of the biggest I've ever climbed over!'

'What's your goalkeeper like?'

'Blind as a bat! He can't even see the ball when it's coming straight at him!'

'That's nothing. Ours can't even find it when it's in the net!'

My home town has a great football team. Last season they lost ten games in a row, but were they discouraged? No! They went right out and lost ten more!

One of the England players, who shall be nameless, had made the acquaintance of a young lady in the lobby of the hotel at which he was staying. He invited her to dinner and spent the entire meal regaling her with anecdotes about his prowess on the field, and how he had held the team together in the most crucial games. As coffee was being served, he said, 'But that's enough about me. Let's talk about you. Tell me, what did you think of my game in the match against Italy?'

There's only one difference today between a professional football player and an amateur, according to a cynic of my acquaintance: the professional gets paid by cheque.

A group of flies were playing football in a saucer, using a lump of sugar as a ball. One of them said, 'We'll have to do better than this, lads – we're playing in the cup tomorrow!'

Referees do very well financially at Leeds United matches. They get 5p back on every bottle.

Boss: 'Why are you so late for work?'
Employee: 'Sorry, boss. I dreamed I was watching the Cup Final and it ran into extra time.'

A lucky fellow recently won £250,000 on the football pools and bought a large public-house in south London. He announced his intention of having it completely redecorated from top to bottom, and on the day the work was completed a large crowd gathered outside at opening time. Suddenly the door opened, and there was the pools winner clutching a pint of beer and accompanied by a very curvaceous blonde.

'What time do you open, mate?' shouted a voice from the crowd.

'Open?' said the pools winner. 'What are you talking about? I bought this place for myself!'

Paddy spread the newspaper out on the table and turned the pages until he came to the 'Spot-the-Ball' competition. He studied the picture carefully, then, taking a pin, he proceeded to prick the picture in an orderly manner.

'What are you doing, Paddy?' asked his room-mate, Mick.

'Trying to find the ball,' said Paddy.

'With a pin? How can you do it with a pin?' asked Mick.

'Well, you keep pricking the paper until you hear a hissing noise. Then you know you've punctured the ball, and there you are!'

Two girls were discussing their local football team. 'I've been out with every member of the Rovers and I haven't made love to one of them!' said one.

'Ah!' said her friend. 'I'll bet it was that shy goalkeeper!'

'Was it a good match this afternoon?' one hooligan asked another.

'Yeah – great!' said his mate. 'Ten arrests, three cars wrecked, a running battle with the police and the referee had his arm broken!'

It's said that everyone is football-mad in Scunthorpe. It's quite true, but then they've got a lot to be mad about.

There's a pub near Arsenal's Highbury stadium where every Saturday night, as regular as clockwork, there are scenes of mayhem and bloodshed as the fans discuss the afternoon's match. A local walked in one Sunday lunchtime and said, in surprise, 'Hey, landlord, what's the idea of putting sawdust all over the floor?'

'That's not sawdust,' said the landlord. 'That's Saturday night's furniture.'

A home supporter staggered into a bar after a Cup match between Walsall and visiting Spurs. 'How did it go?' asked the barman.

'Spurs 15, Walsall nil,' gasped the fan. 'And we were damn lucky to get nil!'

First seagull: 'That's Wembley stadium down there – the Cup Final's just started. Look – there's Paul Gascoigne!'
Second seagull: 'Where? I can't see him.'
First seagull: 'Yes, there he is – I'll spot him for you!'

One famous English international was known to his fellow-players as 'V-Neckline'. He was always plunging down the middle but he rarely showed anything interesting.

A Coventry fan, discussing his team in the local, remarked, 'Dobson would be a good player if it weren't for two things.'

'What are those?' asked a bystander.

'His feet!'

I read a report last week of a keen football fan who had his new baby christened Maradona Dalglish Gascoigne Pele. I think the poor girl's going to be in trouble later in life.

'What did the manager say to you last Saturday when you let in three own goals?'

'Shall I leave out the swear words?'

'Yes.'

'He didn't say anything.'

'I hear you were playing football last Sunday, my son.'

'That's right, vicar. It's not a sin to play football on the Sabbath, is it?'

'It is, the way you play it.'

'What did you think of my game today, coach?'

'Not bad – but I still prefer football.'

The village team had finished bottom of the league for the tenth consecutive year, and as two supporters walked away from the last match of the season, one remarked, 'Well, there's one thing you must say about our boys – they're good losers!'

'Good?' exclaimed his friend. 'They're perfect!'

'How was the match, dear?' asked the wife of a football fan who had just returned home.

'The other side won,' he grumbled. 'By seven very lucky goals!'

A leading footballer died and went to Heaven. At the impressive gates an angel checked his record while St Peter chatted to him. 'I see you're a footballer,' said St Peter, 'and judging by your reports, a very good one.'

'Well,' replied the footballer, 'I did represent my country a number of times.'

'I'm sure you'd like to see our football facilities,' went on St Peter. 'Come on – I'll show them to you.'

When they reached the ground the footballer was amazed at the wonderful facilities. A number of players were at practice and one of them was running around busily shouting instructions and giving advice to the others. The footballer said, 'Who does he think he is? God?'

'He *is* God,' whispered St Peter. 'But he thinks he's Paul Gascoigne!'

The selection committee members were discussing the performances of their players. 'Now we come to the goalkeeper, Nick Fanshawe,' said the chairman. 'What are your views on him?'

'As a goalkeeper,' snorted one member, 'I think Venus de Milo could do a better job!'

'It's obvious why we got beaten last Saturday. The referee comes from the same town as the visiting team.'

'Well, it's only natural, then, isn't it? He's got to travel back in the same train with them.'

An avid football fan turned up at a match between Falkirk and Raith Rovers and proffered £3 to the ticket-seller. 'It's £6 to get in,' said the clerk.

'That's all right,' said the Scotsman. 'I'm a Falkirk supporter – I'll only be watching me own lads!'

A very keen football supporter visited a psychiatrist who was also a fanatical follower of the game. 'I'm going to give you an idea-association test,' said the psychiatrist. 'Now tell me – what is it that has smooth curves and tends to become uncontrollable at crucial moments?'

'A football,' said the patient.

'Good! And what do you think of when two arms slip around your waist?'

'An illegal tackle.'

'Excellent! And what sort of picture comes into your mind

at the mention of a pair of round firm thighs?'

'A World Cup footballer.'

'Very good indeed! Your reactions are perfectly normal. But I'll tell you one thing – you'd be surprised at some of the silly answers I get!'

A very noisy home supporter kept disagreeing vociferously with every decision the referee made. In the end the ref couldn't stand it any longer. He marched over to the stands and shouted up at the offender, 'Who's refereeing this match – you or me?'

'Neither of us!' came the prompt reply.